Searching for Home: Indiana Poems

Scott Sprunger

Copyright © 2012 Scott Sprunger

All rights reserved.

ISBN-13:978-1481208314
ISBN-10:1481208314

DEDICATION

To Indiana……….it's home

Blue Buttons 1945

Sunday afternoon,

Mid-September, clouds pregnant

With life, hung in the autumn air.

She rested in a walnut rocker,

The one her grandfather crafted

From local stock before leaving

Liverpool.
The weathered porch groaned

With each gentle rock of her feet.

Dull nails on parchment

Hands, caressed canary colored correspondence.

Towering trees of Central France closed in

Behind her eyes.

A hawk fastidiously circled

In and out of her son's

Vacant stare.

It was there

That a single sniper,

Wearing one loafer,

Cradled in the arms of an oak,

Called out, squeezing the life

From her only child.

Her right forefinger traced
Circles on the blue, satin
Button at her throat.
The print of mountain flowers rose
And fell with each hitch of her breath.
After school hours at Miller's Mill,
And a birthday trip to Barrett's Five and Dime.

A grin above a chiseled chin,
As she sowed the field of white buds
On a navy blue backing.

Her Sunday best for 150 church meetings,
Committed to continue until he came home.

In a few weeks, when the leaves dance
Across the yard,
And her shawl hugs her
Shoulders,
She will nestle the dress and its blue buttons,
Under his right arm
To be blanketed by the Stars and Bars,
For eternity.

My Life in Shades of Green

Resting in a field of knee high wheat,
The white house with green shutters winked
In the July sun.
Monarch and Swallowtails bounced lazily
Through the humid air in front of me,
Just off a dirt road in Adams County Indiana.

The crumbled first step of the front porch
Greeted me; it had once been my seat
During a family portrait.
The field had been bluegrass then,
A blanket where we picnicked and wrestled.

Stepping onto the rotted floorboards, my reading corner cried
Out to me.
Thunderstorms rolling in from Ohio
Would beat the dust into the road,
While I sat with my back pressed to the house,
Leaves of Grass open before me.

And there it was.
The brass knob.

The brass knob that sang in the sun,
A star in broad daylight

A signal to where my life began.

The brass knob a young man had installed,
Getting everything just right
Before he brought his bride home.

The brass knob my brother had chipped
His right front tooth on,
Kissing home during a game of tag.

The brass knob Grandpa would jiggle,
Just before turning,
So that we kids were ready with a hug.

The brass knob a warning hung from
When a doctor from the county
Deemed my sister's death as Scarlet Fever.

The brass knob I would turn slowly
After midnight,
The scent of her perfume still on my collar.

The brass knob that now lay stiff,
And several shades of green.
As my fingers trembled, the tips
Just brushing its cold shape;
My heart began to cry.

A thousand Sunday dinners,
Every Christmas celebration,
My brother's wedding,
My sister's wake
Had all begun and ended with its smooth turn.

As the tears filled my eyes,
I pulled away from it;
Afraid to release the memories
That it had not already allowed
Me to see.

One Moment

Red cheek weather
And Grandpa's chili.
Autumn's fallen soldiers
Kiss my mother's headstone.

Hot, thick, wool pants;
Red and gray hunting socks.
New rubber boots with Indiana clay
Swallowing their
Soles.

Patience.
Deer hide gloves
Gripping, squeezing,
A pheasant cartwheels through a puddle.
It stops to stare at its refection in a
Dented, scarred hubcap near
My foot.

Mona Lee

And Mona Lee sighed,
Her tired eyes reflecting the years.
Across her lap laid her life,
A faded quilt carefully folded.
Her swollen feet began to rock her,
To rock her back to when they were all young.
Tatters of all things that made her Mona Lee
Bound together, united
To remind her to never forget the times
She laughed, cried, and mostly loved.

First, a pink cloud of cotton,
Little Angelica's sleeper.
Visions of a curly blonde gift from God
And the giggles that echoed through her dreams.
The sadness of holding her and knowing
One day she would grow up to leave and live
Her own memories.

Next, a weather stained twill named Jacksonville Johnnie.
He had come to chop wood and play peek-a-boo from
Behind the pines with Angelica.
Quiet, conservative Johnnie.
The one with stubble and his right incisor split.
He had stayed through August, into September

Until the trees put on their annual show
Of color and romance.
One last wink at his blonde friend,
He lowered his head and shuffled down the lane.

A square of Olive Drab lay next to Johnnie.
That was redheaded Eddie, two houses over.
His freckled face would appear at the screen door,
The scent of Mona's cookies drifting through.
He had looked so handsome in his gray suit
The night he walked her little girl to the Senior Ball.
He had slightly stammered on bended knee,
Taking her Angelica, heart and soul, for his own.
He had broken that heart when he stayed in
Southeast Asia, his body never found.

And so it continued, as it did every night,
Mona's shaking hands touching each square,
The longing for the past growing stronger,
As she said goodnight to all of those
Who had made her life her own.

Moonlight Serenade

Her hands shook
As he, in an Olive Drab jacket and khaki slacks,
Placed the gold band on her finger,
Promising forever.

Her hands kissed his,
Her blue cotton dress pressed
To his chest,
Her smile tilted to the sky,
As they swirled, and stirred,
To the echoes of Glenn Miller in the maples,
Under a Harvest Moon, through the headlights
Of his De Soto.

Her hands held him close,
A smoking unfiltered Camel to her lips,
A radio reporting
News of Europe as the wind howled against the window panes
And his son slept in a white bassinet in the front room.

Her hands wrung her lace
Handkerchief, while sitting on an oak folding chair,
Wearing perfume and real nylons,
The lone sound of a trumpet calling
To the granite stones.

Her hands remembered
Slowly tracing the lines of the hood
On the monument to their love,
A gray decaying De Soto on the banks of the Wabash,
Its headlights blinding staring
At the horizon.

It's grinning grille
And off white interior hugged
Her during late nights
When loneliness had stole her slumber.

It's pitted chrome trim reflected
The light that danced in his eyes
When he had kneeled in the damp grass taking
Her hand in his, and whispered the words that stole
Her heart.

Calls from a Blue Jay would follow
Her through the grass field in spring,
The dusty brown trail wove
To her Fountain of Youth,
When time stood still,
And old love woke from its dreams.

At last,
Her hands lay folded,

Resting,

While a man wearing an orange cap scratched his head and stared

At the woman wearing a blue cotton dress,

Photos of a soldier, and an infant lying

Next to a half pack of Camels on the backseat,

Her smile tilted once more to the sky.

Summer Song 1977

The haze of 3AM lurks
In my head.
Spiderman sheets tangle
Between skinned shins draping
Over Tonka trucks on the floor.

White ceiling glowing
From a single street lamp,
The metallic bounce
Of a beetle on my screen.

Stale scent of menthols ride
A summer breeze through
The window carrying
Mumbles and stifled laughs
From two friends sitting
In pink lawn chairs.

Their words run
Over me like bath water massaging
Me back to sleep.

November 14ᵗʰ (in the rain)

My fingers traced lines
in the dust from C.R. 35,
that had followed me by clinging
to my black shoes.
A white cotton cloth bathed and erased
all but the finality of the day.
My rumpled coat carried no program,
my hands bore no blood.

She wore a cotton print,
gold rimmed glasses with a chip
in the right lens.
There were no children,
no red-eyed loved ones perched in pews of oak.
Only two graying deacons,
a janitor wearing a silk rose,
and me.

My eyes moved across her spotted forehead,
had she once been beautiful?
An Indiana rose wound around a fence post
along a field of freshly plowed earth.

Had this woman with the mole sleeping on her right cheek
once been my neighbor? Never pulling the weeds

from her daffodils but always hiding

behind a sign that begs

"No Soliciting"?

Had she sat in a walnut rocker

knitting, tears filling the folds of her face as she looked at a faded photograph sitting on the mantel,

while she thought of morning talks over eggs and wheat toast?

Had she thought of this day

when she would sleep in her Sunday best,

a preacher speaking to the walls around her

and strangers walked her last steps?

I watched a digger named Bud throw the first shovel of clay.

I turned slowly, walked down the gravel road,

red eyes to the sky

as this woman with no name faded into the earth

and a love for her burned in my heart.

Two August Days

He held the cardboard above his head,
A puddle forming over his crude lettering.
The drops mixed with tears
Blending with the salt and pepper patch
On his cheek.
A veteran of concrete doorways and
Beat cops,
His pack lie resting
Between two worn Jungle Boots.

Our eyes met for an instant.
I, the young man he once was;
Him, the broken man I never hoped to be.
I felt his pain,
A thousand hungry days,
Empty pockets and shattered dreams.
My foolish youth, his blood stained wisdom.
My visions of hope and glory,
His memories of death and his inability to forget.
My starched white shirt and blue tie screamed
At his greasy jeans and his moth-eaten field parka.
My fear of looking; his bravery in searching
For a youth lost in the twitch of a finger.

In a blink, he looked away.

I drove on; relieved that I was no
Longer scrutinized by a stare.

Among those I love, I often think of him
Shivering in the snow and thinking of me.
I longed to help him, he wished to save me.

To save me from the world I so desperately fight to compete in.
The same world that made him a man
In the jungle grass on another August day;
His visions of hope and glory destroyed.

Yesterday's Never Gone

It was past the time when the hour hand's
Revolutions were painted with tears.
It was past the moment when a single red rose,
Resting on oak, lowered itself to be covered
In Indiana clay.
It was closer to the days,
Those days,
When I sat among scattered papers,
Cigarette butts and torn photographs.

I could feel loneliness the way I could smell
Spring coming to Madison.
The mist from Big Clifty clinging to a moss
Eaten maple.
Laughter bellowing from the sandstone that
Framed the sleeping brook.
March air kissing red cheeks,
Hearts skipping beats, in love with life.

I stared out the west window for years.
There was the hill we once sat on in the
Shade of an oak.
A blue, wool blanket pressing the crabgrass
Flat while we talked, chuckled, remembered.
Ants formed a conga line to my ham and

Cheese sandwich,
The way tears licked their way to the
Corners of her smile when I bit into it.

The path that runs through the chicken yard,
The path that crosses the Kissing Bridge,

That path that creeps past the rotted Model A
Ford that hobos sometimes sleep in.
The path when I bring her flowers,
The path that leads to the chipped, rusty back
Gate and a sign that reads
Rosewood Cemetery.

It was long after we said "I do" in a white
Washed church with no steeple
To a preacher wearing a black tie.
It was past the time when I sat among the
Cattails holding a lace handkerchief bearing
"J.S." in one corner,
While slowly turning my gold wedding band
Between scarred fingers.

It was when I fell between the snow peas and
The sweet corn,
My overalls stained in black earth,
Wind burning the lower lids of my eyes,

That I saw her standing near the porch,

Where she'd always been,

Wearing a cotton dress,

Hanging my shirts on the line.

No Harvest

An Ohio Blue Tip is flicked to life in a field of uncut wheat.
Cupped by a bulging hand covered in ashen hair,
it's raised to meet a Lucky and a deep breath.
Smoke lingers,
then dives into the wrinkles brought on by sixty-seven summers.
Eyes of sapphire stare out across the field,
fixed on a clump of maples near the west road.

Those eyes.
America's eyes.
His eyes.

His eyes have felt the sting of sweat
and the cutting edge of the harrow's reins
as two nags led him across the earth.
His eyes have worried through framed glass,
darkness,
hail dancing on the tin roof.
His eyes wept under a September sun
as his son's blood drained into the grass
from beneath an overturned John Deere.
His eyes laughed when Old Roy sprouted
quills from the end of his snout.
His eyes questioned the skies
when they brought no rain and the dirt rose like a ghost and flew away.

His eyes turned bitter when fields of towering corn were crushed
beneath the pavement of a new shopping mall.
His eyes choked for breath when a pink slip from the auditor
shoved them into the red.
His eyes trembled as a man in a gray suit
beat an auction sign into the yard using his worn shovel.
His eyes dimmed as friends and strangers roamed his farm looking for treasures.

His eyes died
as he cast away the Lucky
into a field of uncut wheat,
turned and crept back to his home
within the city limits.

Luther's Progress

Going to Edgerton on the left there is a barn.
Its high walls grin, its incisors gone.
The moss covered planks that once made
The wall a sheet of raw, red tradition were
Used (by a man named Luther)
For the tailgate of a '53 Ford truck.
The truck that kicks up dust in the fields
As the young men gather the rocks that
Could chip the harrows blade.

The roof has the remains of a tobacco ad
Still clinging to it.
There is a rectangular gap where the "A"
In "Mail Pouch" should be,
Sparrows know this as an escape route,
A gateway to safety from the bite of a
Daisy Rough Rider.
Bits of straw and string form a border to
The hole.

In the yard stands the windmill.
Its gears welded together by the absence of
Oil and human touch.
Its frame is still strong. Tornadoes,
Bolts of lightning, and twelve gauge slugs

Could not bring it down.
A hook sings against the steel supports.
The spot is shiny silver while the rest has
Surrendered to a dirty red.
It was hung there in the '30's for Luther
And his dad to hang their deer to bleed out.

There is no house here. Once it was a rose
Among the thistles on this
Ohio dirt farm.
The porch hugged the kitchen and family
Room windows.
Luther would set on the steps
Counting stars while his father listened
To Amos and Andy on their Philco.
Those same steps set just south of the old barn.
Nestled in dandelions, they lie in the sun,
Feeling naked without the warmth of
A family planted behind them.

To Remember

The mosquitoes will be gone in a few days,
But they leave welts on my arm as a remembrance.
The sun bites my eyes from the waters edge,
Almost forcing me inside,
Almost.
Doll sized oaks swim in their mothers discarded dress,
Former tadpoles belch from the far side of the pond.

The windmill that grew twelve gauge slug
Sized holes,
Lies rusting between a '42 Plymouth and an
'83 Mustang.
Five kittens form a sea of fur at my feet.
Their mother chews at a flea that is kissing
Her left hip.

The shadows divide the reds
In the pile of deer gears
That lie near the eight pointer known as My first.

On my grandson's Opening Day,
I'll remember a tremor as I fired that day.
And upon remembering
He will be elder
Despite my ancient face.

Searching for Home

Home had been a small Indiana town,
One stoplight, a dime store,
And a grocery where the keeper knew my name.

Home had been Little League games
Under dusty lights in June skies,
Parents calling from the bleachers,
Pepsi's and popcorn in their fists.

Home had been where mother called
For dinner,
Sunny Saturdays with the smell of charcoal
And laughter as horse shoes clanged against steel posts.

Home had been eight thousand miles
From dripping jungle leaves,
Burning straw huts,
And black nights with red tracer fire.

Home drew closer each moment,
As big cities fell behind me,
The sun set before my face,
And the dust of Southeast Asia shook from my shoulders.

Midwestern corn fields melted

Into manicured lawns,
Mailboxes with red flags standing,
A flashing light at a crossroads winked
At me and kept time
With the beat of my heart.

There, angry words of men cut me.
Murderer, baby killer, this is what I am to them.
Lingering stares of housewives holding shopping bags catch
The tears that slide into my beard.
My youth was traded for their freedom,
And they hate me for it.
This is not home.

Home is where the dime sized drops of rain bathe
The toes of my boots.
Cracked asphalt sliding beneath me,
And the ancient smell of sunrise greets me
While crossing the eastern train tracks at the edge of town.
Houses with sleepy windows, and
Silent dogs on heavy chains slip by
As I make my way through the rain,
To where I can shed my pack,
And with open arms,
Embrace the place of my birth
And hearing it whisper,
"Welcome Home son."

The Photo Shoot

"Ready?" her crouching husband called. Their son, Willie, stood by her side, playing with Roscoe their Weiner dog. She wore a sweater, and had insisted the guys wore jackets. The bright sky had the crisp bite of autumn in it, and meant only one thing there in Auburn: the Fair was coming.

"Smile". The camera flashed, its white light blinding her.

Suddenly there was her husband, still crouching, but this time younger, wearing his favorite denim jacket, his hair longer and fuller. They had just picnicked under a large oak near the Spencerville Covered Bridge. Slowly he reached into the pocket and pulled out the simple gold band and held it up to her. She had cried, nodded her head, and placed her hand outward…..

Flash!

holding the results of her pregnancy test. They had been told they would never have children. She had been sick every morning for weeks, and this seemed to be the next logical step. A trip to the drugstore, and a ten minute wait while it processed. She raised it so they both could see. Her husband cried out "Woohoo! We did it! We're having a…."

Flash!

"puppy!" Willie squealed. The dark brown Dachshund puppy wearing the red ribbon on its collar yipped and licked the five year olds face. They became a tangle of child, brown fur, giggles and yips as they quickly became friends.

Delighted Willie began to make a list, " We need a leash, an' a bowl, an' a ball. Oh Mommy, we don't have…."

Flash!

"much time." The doctor frowned. "I'm very sorry".

Tears filling their eyes, together they asked, "How long?"

"Maybe 3 months."He paused. "I suggest you make the most memories you can with what time you have left. I'll give you two a few moments alone." He left the office and their world shrank around them. They held each other, grasping for each moment they had spent together, reaching for the memories not yet made, and struggled to accept that they would never see one another grow old as they had always planned.

They had decided only to tell Willie that Mommy would be going away for awhile but before she did, they wanted to do all sorts of things together. Willie had frowned when he thought of his mother going on a trip, but a wide eyed smile crossed his face when he thought of all the things they could do before she went. "Adventures!" He had grinned.

There had been a trip to the zoo, a big league ball game, the beach, and a long weekend of camping where they had cooked all of their meals over a fire. Last was the trip to her hometown so Willie could see where she had grown up.

She remembered running down the sidewalks of downtown after school, the very ones they were posing on now. She would fly down Seventh Street, her white Keds pounding on the pavement. She would turn right, and Mrs. Moore would be walking Lilly at the corner of 6th and Main. "Hi Lilly!" she would call as she sailed by.

Further down the block across the street sat Mary in front of her neighbor's deli eating a sandwich. Her mother was a painter and had been commissioned to paint a picture of the Eckhart Library. She needed the evening light to paint by for the mood to be "just right" so Mary had to wait until after dark for actual supper. The sandwich was a little something to tide her over.

At this point she would nearly be out of breath as she bounded up the steps to the old YMCA. She would spend her time swimming, and maybe playing basketball if the big kids would let her. She had always dreamed of being in the Olympics, and she knew she had to be in tip top shape if she were to make it.

The memory caused her to close her eyes as a cool breeze blew her hair across her face. Smiling, she brushed the hair and the memory from her face, and looked at her husband still kneeling on the sidewalk in front of her.

"Haven't you taken enough pictures here?" she laughed.

"Never" he smiled. "One more". He fiddled with the focus. "Smile!"

A small click but the blink of bright light from the flash was missing. He turned the camera over and bit his lip, "Oh, we're out of film" he frowned.

And nearly out of time, she thought. Her hands drew Willie close, and while hugging him, she closed her eyes, the small smile still on her lips.

Made in the USA
Charleston, SC
05 July 2013